Wildlife of the Land's End Peninsula

An Introduction to the Natural History of the Land's End Peninsula

107201

914·237

COR

Contents

The main part of the text was contributed by Roger Burrows, Tutor in Natural History in the Extra-Mural Department of Exeter University.

The section on Visiting and Migrant birds was contributed by Roger Butts, a local representative in Cornwall of the Royal Society for the Protection of Birds.

Published by Cornwall County Council.
ISBN 0 902319 20 5

011346

West Penwith, more familiarly known as the Land's End peninsula, is an area of unique and outstanding beauty. Isolated as Britain's south-western extremity, this great granite promontory is almost an island, its only link to the mainland a strip of low lying and marshy land just four miles wide between Marazion and Hayle. From St. Ives around to Mousehole the whole of the magnificent thirty-three mile coast, with its high cliffs and sandy coves backed by rugged tor capped moorland, has been recognised by the Countryside Commission as one of the country's 'Heritage Coasts.' This title is reserved for those stretches of coast of exceptionally fine scenery, unspoiled character and possessing a wealth of heritage features.

Heritage Coasts deserve special measures to conserve their quality and resist the growing and unprecedented pressures which threaten to destroy their character. The West Penwith Heritage Coast is no exception, and both the Cornwall County Council and Penwith District Council are taking action to help ensure this protection. However, an understanding of nature by the public as a whole, supported by an appreciation of the vulnerability of our environment, is the real key to effective conservation. The aim of this book, therefore, is to provide a guide to just one aspect of West Penwith's rich heritage—its wildlife; the wealth of both its flora and fauna and the widely contrasting habitats to be found within this sixty-six square mile peninsula.

Produced by the Countryside Projects Section of the Cornwall County Planning Department.

1

Introduction – Geology, Land Form and Climate

The Land's End peninsula rises abruptly from the Atlantic, cliffs of granite over 200 feet high face the south and west, while to the north the coast is the finest example in England and Wales of cliffs cut in metamorphic rock. Above the cliffs the land abruptly flattens to a high table land carved by the sea about half a million years ago. In the southern half of the peninsula the ground rises only gently, but along the north coast the country is higher and more desolate. A range of tor capped granite hills run parallel to the north coast, rising to 826 feet at Watch Croft, east of Morvah, and 812 feet at the tor topped Trendrine Hill, east of Zennor.

Many millions of years ago the granite of Land's End, now exposed in cliff and tor, formed the core of a high mountain chain which stretched from the present day Isles of Scilly, through Cornwall and

HOR POINT.

Devon, to Brittany and beyond. Deep down the hot granite magma cooled slowly and large crystals of white felspar, black mica and colourless quartz crystallised to give the now familiar black and white of granite. It has been exposed for us to see by millions of years of erosion by the elements and by changes in sea level which, about half a million years ago, left the area as a granite island similar to those now forming the Isles of Scilly. In fact if the present day sea level rose a few feet the island would re-form, with the sea stretching from Hayle in the north to Marazion in the south.

Erosion lowered the old mountains, removing thousands of feet of sediment, until the cores of the uplands were all that was left; it is these old mountain roots that we now see when we look at the granite cliffs and hills.

Erosion has also produced the piles of flat jointed granite which look sometimes like man-made structures perched on top of the northern hills of the area. These 'tors' are reflected in the truly man-made Megalithic structures such as Lanyon Quoit of about 2,000 B.C. but the tors are millions, rather than thousands of years old and were there long before Stone Age man arrived.

Man has farmed the area for many centuries as the ancient 'celtic' field pattern near Zennor shows, with its stone enclosed small fields dating from the Bronze Age. The loose granite boulders which once covered the soil were built into neat stone walls which in Cornwall are known as 'hedges'. The Cornish hedges are a dominant feature of the peninsula and give it part of its unique character.

Where it outcrops in the cliffs and hill

2

tops the granite is well jointed often in three directions at right angles roughly to each other. This results in the characteristic piled block appearance of the weathered granite producing the famous castle-like or castellated cliffs of the south and west coast. Often the slightly softer layers weather quickly and leave great perched blocks on a small plinth, as at the famous rocking or Logan Stone, near Treen. To the north a succession of headlands, coves and clefts, known locally as 'zawns' have been cut into the hard metamorphic rock or 'killas'. This rock once formed a complete fringe to the granite, but has now been largely eroded away.

It is to the granite that the rich mineral deposits of West Penwith owe their origin. Many of the old mine heaps are still obvious and uncovered by vegetation. This is largely due to the high toxic mineral content and lack of covering soil, the high rainfall here not being conducive to the accumulation of

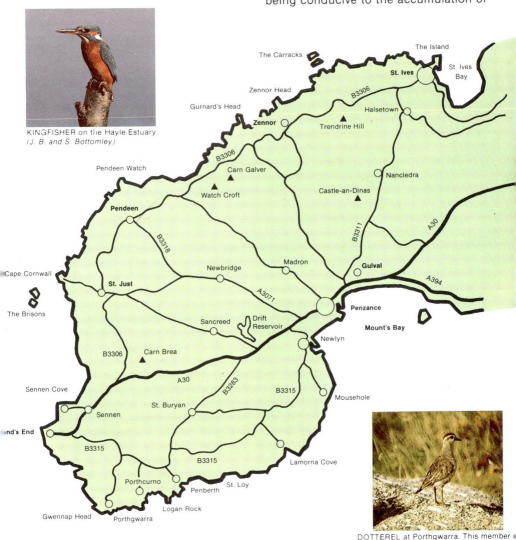

KINGFISHER on the Hayle Estuary. (J. B. and S. Bottomley)

DOTTEREL at Porthgwarra. This member of the plover family is a rare passage migrant in Cornwall. (J. B. and S. Bottomley)

3

BUZZARD; a common sight, soaring on broad motionless wings over the clifftops and moorland. (Eric and David Hosking)

BUFF-BREASTED SANDPIPER at Porthgwarra; a 'vagrant' carried across the Atlantic by cross-winds while on migration. (J. B. and S. Bottomley)

soil in crevices. Mosses and fern do, however, partly obscure the old mine waste and sea pink occasionally thrives.

The weathered, honey-coloured granite cliffs form the first mainland obstacle to the massive swell of the Atlantic. The pulverising effect of the Atlantic breakers on granite has produced a pale, maize-coloured and shell rich sand, giving the clear sea its intense blueness even on an overcast day.

Land's End takes the full brunt of the wind sweeping in across thousands of miles of open sea to produce the famous surf of Sennen Cove. It is these same winds which bring some unusual species to Great Britain including migrating birds blown off course from North America; these find a first landfall at coves such as

Porthgwarra. The North American monarch butterfly sometimes arrives along the south coast, it too having had a wind assisted passage. It is suspected that some birds and even butterflies hitch a lift on shipping, for this is a busy seaway.

Exposure to the south-west wind has given the landscape a relatively treeless appearance, woodland being confined to the sheltered valleys. However, it can hardly be claimed that the dominant wind direction is at present from the south-west, as for a number of years both easterly and northerly elements have increased in the wind patterns. The far south-west can now expect winters with lower temperatures bringing frost and snow to an area which formerly was

FOXGLOVE WITH RED CAMPION;
flowers June-September.
SCURVY GRASS; flowers May-August.

FOX CUB near Zennor; the boulder strewn
moorland and derelict mine workings provide
ideal cover for the fox. *(J. B. and S. Bottomley)*

noted for its mild, wet, misty winters. However, the warm Gulf Stream waters coming up from the South Atlantic, still wash against the peninsula and at Land's End this warm current divides, sending one part of the North Atlantic Drift up the western coast of the British Isles , and another along the English Channel. These waters bring a variety of marine animals with them in the form of floating jellyfish, swimming turtles, dolphins and fish, including the formerly abundant pilchard, once the basis of major fishery in the area. Warm waters also mean sharks; these great fish range from the fish-eating varieties, such as the blue and the thresher, to the gigantic—up to forty feet—plankton-eating basking shark. Basking sharks can sometimes be seen cruising close to shore in summer, straining the small planktonic animals and plants from the sea in their huge open mouths.

Despite the colder winters, the area can still expect higher temperatures compared with the rest of the mainland, and relatively few frosty days, frost seldom lingering after sunrise. Summers tend to be cooler than in less maritime areas and the cliffs and higher moorland are often shrouded in a white blanket of drifting sea mist.

It is the combination of mildness and dampness, together with the salt-laden spray and the often searing wind, which moulds the vegetation of the area and determines the nature of its animal populations.

Cliff and Cove

The cliffs once formed the traditional home of the Cornish chough but no longer echo to its harsh calls, as the bird is now extinct as a truly wild bird in this county. Its place has, in part, been taken by the abundant jackdaws which breed along the cliffs and in the ruined engine houses of the old mines. Ravens are fairly common, and carrion crows often feed along the strand line on the shore, performing with the other crows aerial acrobatics or, conversely, hanging almost motionless in the strong updrafts of wind coming off the sea. Fulmars, herring gulls, great black-backed gulls and the less common lesser black-backed gull can also be seen riding the thermals.

Further out to sea gannets, shearwaters and petrels ride the troughs and peaks of the swell and breaking water. Kittiwakes are common, and a glimpse of a peregrine falcon is always possible. Few breeding sea birds will be found between Sennen and Cape Cornwall but they do breed on many other areas of the mainland cliff. Fulmars are most common between Porthgwarra and Sennen, and in the same area will be found kittiwake and herring gull colonies and a few breeding great black-backed gulls. A few auks breed on the mainland cliffs but most occur on the offshore islands such as The Brisons, off Cape Cornwall, and The Armed Knight, off Land's End. The Brisons have the largest razorbill colony in Cornwall and another auk, the guillemot, shares the breeding ledges. The sea around The Brisons was one of the most badly affected by oil and detergent in 1967 from the Torrey Canyon incident, and the resident bird population suffered accordingly.

The steep cliffs and offshore islands of the Land's End peninsula provide ideal breeding sites for the shag whose numbers have been increasing in recent years. The cormorant, a relative of the shag, which is often a freshwater feeder is more usually found around Mount's Bay in the south and the Hayle estuary in the north.

All around the cliffs the diminutive dark rock pipit will be seen feeding, often in company with oystercatchers and turnstones on exposed rocks.

Kestrels hover above the low vegetation of the cliff top looking for field and bank voles which are abundant. They are less likely to catch the more nocturnal woodmouse which also makes its home amongst the roots and branches of the wind sculpted low shrubs and coarse grasses.

Buzzards are a common sight, soaring and circling above their intended victims. Once principally dependent on rabbits, now, following the outbreak of myxomatosis in the 1950s, buzzards feed mainly on small mammals, birds and even adders. The smaller cliff top birds such as stonechat, wren, linnet and meadow pipit and much rarer cirl bunting are more vulnerable to the low swooping rushes of the sparrowhawk.

Adders usually bask on open rocks or in sunny hollows, a habitat they share with the common lizard, which can be seen easily if cautiously approached. Slow worms, which are actually legless lizards, commonly occur under any protective stone or fallen stump of gorse. Harmless grass snakes, with their characteristic yellow collar behind the head, frequent the wetter areas where they often take frogs and the now more abundant toads.

The Cornwall Coast Path can be followed right round the peninsula and is by far

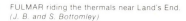
FULMAR riding the thermals near Land's End.
(J. B. and S. Bottomley)

the best way to see the area in detail.
Mammal predators, while common are
seldom seen except by the early footpath
walker. These include fox, badger, and
the latter's smaller relatives, the stoat and
weasel. The large semi-aquatic otter, also
of the weasel family, was formerly
common but is now a rarity. All take a
heavy toll of the small rodents, and
occasionally eat the common and pygmy
shrew whose shrieking fights can often
be heard on a clifftop walk during the
summer.

After the birds, the insects are perhaps
the most conspicuous of the clifftop
animals. Here will be found common
blue, green hairstreak, small copper and
grayling butterflies. Moths are
represented by day-flying Burnet moths,
the conspicuous black and yellow
caterpillars of which often devastate the
cliff ragwort. Those of the drinker moth
and the oak eggar are commonly seen
but the green, yellow and black emperor
moth caterpillars are less often found.
The drinker and oak eggar moths fly
mostly at night as does the magnificent
emperor moth, but the latter can
sometimes be seen resting during the
day on the heather.

During the summer large numbers of
silvery moths occur along the cliffs to
which they migrate from the Continent,
while in the rocky coves it is often
possible to watch butterflies arriving or
departing, flying low and seeming
perilously close to a salt water end.
Brimstones, clouded yellows, painted
ladies, red admirals, small tortoiseshell
and peacocks can all be seen in this way.

Bush crickets can sometimes be heard
in the evenings and grasshoppers are a
constant daytime member of the clifftop
heathland and grassland populations.

ADDER: common on clifftop heaths and
moorland. It feeds mainly on small mammals,
lizards and frogs. (J. B. and S. Bottomley)

CORMORANT. The cormorant, distinguished by its white throat patch, is greatly outnumbered in this area by the shag. *(F. E. Gibson)*

GREY ATLANTIC SEAL. *(F. E. Gibson)*

Green woodpeckers and cuckoos, although typically woodland birds are often to be found along the coastal heathland.

Flowers can be found at almost any time of the year and during spring and summer the cliffs have a profusion of often brightly coloured flowers, occurring in thousands to form large splashes of colour on the cliff slopes. The flower cover is of vernal squill, kidney vetch, and bird's-foot trefoil, sea campion, sea mayweed, stonecrop, violet, betony, lousewort, saw-wort, wild thyme (often on ant hills), wood sage, milkwort, primroses and the scrambling madder plus the locally common parasitic plant, dodder.

Nearer the edge of the cliffs, often in

SHAG. *(J. B. and S. Bottomley)*

reach of constant salt spray, are the more truly maritime plants such as common and Danish scurvy grass, samphire of both common and golden varieties, sea beet, sea and buck's-horn plantain and the attractive rock sea lavender, rock sea spurry, Burnet rose, and wild carrot, with perhaps the most abundant and widespread of the maritime plants, sea pink, occurring in great rounded cushions.

Flowering plants do not have the cliffs to themselves, for a variety of mosses and lichens grow here. Lower down, just above the seaweeds the cliffs are often darkened by the black of the lichen *Verrucaria,* while higher up tufted pale green/grey *Ramalina* shares the rock faces with other lichens of bright yellow, orange or white. It is often lichens which give the colour to the cliffs rather than the rocks themselves and it is sometimes impossible to see any rock showing through the living blanket. This is indicative of a moist and pollution free air. During the autumn the attractive parasol mushroom can be found and large puffballs grow in the springy clifftop grass. Shrubs and ivy occur in crevices along the cliff face, along with our only true maritime fern, the sea spleenwort, which is found within reach of salt spray.

Blackthorn, wind and salt spray trimmed, form dense impenetrable thickets, but along the cliff tops heather and ling, along with the dwarf gorse, provide the dominant shrub population. The taller European gorse is rampant, often forming rank, smothering growths up to ten feet high, a great fire hazard during a dry summer. The gorse or 'furze' as it is called locally, is a fine sight when in full flower.

On the steep cliffs of the North Coast an unusual sight is the presence of feral goats, the now semi-wild descendants of once locally domesticated animals.

As they swim close inshore the grey Atlantic seals may be watched from almost any clifftop vantage point. Individuals are also a common sight close to beaches, resting in their characteristic 'bottling' position with only their heads showing above the surface. On offshore rocky islands, in particular the Carracks near Zennor, seals may be seen in number at almost any time of the year. Once regarded as pests by local fishermen, the seal population is kept in check by a very high mortality rate amongst baby seals during the autumn and winter gales. ›

SEA CAMPION: flowers June–August.

Rocky Shore and Sandy Beach

The constantly moving sand of the open beaches of the peninsula does not provide suitable places for burrowing animals to live and only shells and other animal remains washed in by the waves will be found here. A wide variety of shells can be found, however, from smooth trough shells up to two inches long, to the smallest brightly coloured scallop shell less than a quarter of an inch across. Others include the blue ray limpet, grey top shell, saddle oyster, common and china limpets, edible mussel and dog cockle. Many more varieties will be revealed by carefully searching the sands as the tide retreats.

The rocks surrounding the beach are where the living plants and animals will be found. The wild wave action and presence of many limpets on the rocks prevents much large growth of seaweed taking place. Edible laver and Irish moss do occur, the former mainly in the winter when much sand is removed from the beaches. The rocks then exposed are quickly colonised by this red weed which resembles thin plastic sheeting. Seaweeds such as channel wrack and spiral wrack also occur and, lower down the shore, flat wrack and the large oar weeds appear at, or just above, low tide levels. Rock pools are especially rewarding places to study here; a variety of sea anemones, top shells, periwinkles, prawns and small shore fish share the water with abundant and often beautifully delicate red seaweeds and the larger green sea lettuce. Under loose stones in the pools may be found chitons, sponges, sea squirts and encrusting worms and seamats, together with small hermit and shore crabs, squat lobsters, and Cornish sucker fish. These, despite their name, are not confined to the

Duchy. The strange elongated and well-named pipe fish, the nearest relative we have to the sea horses of warmer waters, can also be discovered here.

Stranded on the beach a variety of exotic plants and animals may be found, from jellyfish such as the Portuguese man-o-war and the transparent 'sails' of the by-the-wind sailor, to the occasional turtle, and much more common goose barnacles attached to floating wood, bottles or even to plastic and old solid lumps of oil.

Tropical beans may wash right across from the West Indies and still germinate, and a flying-fish is by no means impossible to see. The egg cases of skate or dogfish which are commonly known as mermaids' purses, the 'bone' of cuttlefish or the sponge-like egg mass of the edible whelk may also be washed ashore. Plants from deeper water such as the thick tough 'stems' of the oar weed are frequently stranded in great masses after gales and carry, still attached to them, a wide variety of other smaller plants and animals.

There is a need to conserve our shallow water plants and animals. Each year the collection of specimens by skin divers and the accidental pollution of the waters by oil, if only in small quantities, take a heavy toll. Sea urchins which were formerly abundant are now much scarcer due to indiscriminate collection for the holiday souvenir trade which has destroyed the local breeding population.

Top: SCALLOP; note the tube worms encrusting the shell. *(N. J. C. Tregenza)*
Far left: PLUMOSE ANEMONE. *(N. J. C. Tregenza)*
Left: DAHLIA ANEMONE. *(N. J. C. Tregenza)* Despite their name and appearance, sea anemones are in fact animals, all are carnivorous—using their tentacles to catch their food.

Farmland, Hedge and Lane

Small fields surrounded by Cornish hedges of granite blocks, sometimes of huge proportions, are the characteristic landscape feature on the flatter areas of the table land. Dairy farming predominates and pasture is the main agricultural land use. Hedges round pasture fields have only a thin turf cover on top and bare granite sides which show the ancient building skill of the Cornish farmer. Fortunately their construction methods are still being carried on by the Cornwall County Council Highways Department, who build traditional hedges after undertaking road improvement schemes.

The hedgerows support a mass of flowers in spring and summer. At the base grow lesser celandines, violets, red campion, the tall alexanders, hogweed and yarrow. Along the sides the blue flowered sheepsbit, ivy leaved toadflax and ground ivy flourish; even on the bare granite stonecrop and pennywort may be found. During the summer the hedges are often covered with foxgloves, particularly where the soil is disturbed.

The tops of the hedges are seldom covered with shrubs on the north coast, but on the more sheltered south side tall blackthorn, European gorse and elder form windbreaks. From the hedge tops blackthorn often spreads to form dense roadside thickets. Badgers and foxes leave muddy footprints in well marked runway areas over the stone hedges.

During the winter months flocks of redwing and fieldfare arrive from colder northern areas together with lapwing and golden plover and vast flocks of starlings. Throughout the year magpies, carrion crow, rooks, buzzards and kestrels can be seen over or on the fields. At ploughing time the ever present flocks of herring gulls and black-backed gulls plunder the exposed worms and insects. Meadow pipits and larks are common over the fields, and wrens, dunnocks and blackbirds are frequent hedge nesting species. Curlews and snipe visit the wetter pastures in their search for food but seldom breed here.

Speckled wood and wall brown butterflies are found along sheltered lanes and skippers, meadow browns and gatekeepers are all common butterflies of pasture and hedgerow. In the damper areas peacock butterflies are found visiting the flowers of the hemp agrimony.

Mild weather and the clean moist air are to the liking of a wide variety of lichens which festoon trees and shrubs, clothing their branches in pale green ragged sleeves. Orange lichens grow profusely on the slate roofs of farm buildings.

Ferns, particularly common polypody, hard fern, hartstongue and spleenwort grow in abundance along the roadsides and on the hedges.

GRASSHOPPER WARBLER at Porthgwarra. This shy bird remains hidden in thick cover, reluctant to fly.
(J. B. and S. Bottomley)

Valleys

The only easily accessible valleys are those along the south coast. Here they form deep clefts in the high ground of the main land mass and run north-west to south-east, their southern mouths opening to the sea.

Each valley is carved by small streams as at Lamorna, St. Loy, Penberth and Porthcurno. These valleys are thick with trees but even in this sheltered situation their tops are often levelled by the wind and look mechanically trimmed. Each tree provides shelter for the next so the height increases in the wood down wind. Very few of the oaks that probably formed the original tree cover in the area still survive the onslaughts of man and weather. The dominant tree is the small leaved Cornish elm which unfortunately is no more resistant to Dutch elm disease than its larger leaved relatives, and many are dead or dying.

Towards St. Ives and Penzance the trees are much more abundant and varied, the area benefiting from better soils and the sheltering effect of the high ground to the north and west. Beech, chestnut and oak all reach a good size in this area.

The most successful trees are the ash and the sycamore, the former coming into leaf late, whereas the large leaved sycamore is often rapidly denuded of its leaves by early gales. Despite wind, salt and poor soils, both trees multiply quickly, pushing between the great granite boulders of the valley floor and clinging to the more exposed valley sides. Rooks, carrion crows, magpies and mistle thrushes build in the tree cover and treecreepers, wrens, goldcrests, robins, mistle thrushes, song thrushes, and blackbirds commonly feed or nest in the lower shrubs.

Holly is common and great thickets of rhododendron cover the woodland floor as do hazel, and the choking bramble. These, together with the massive growths of bracken fern during the summer, do not facilitate easy access on foot.

Other ferns too grow in abundance, the common polypody is often found growing along the branches of lichen and algae covered elms. Cottages and houses in the valleys frequently grow exotic shrubs such as camellias, japonica, South American escallonia, New Zealand hebe, pittosporum and Japanese euonymus. Dense stands of bamboo are frequently seen providing shelter. Many of the herbs growing in these sheltered areas are either garden escapes or non-native plants. These include the man-made hybrid montbretia, green alkanet, Mexican fleabane, with the giant rhubarb-like gunnera group (in the very wet areas near streams), pink purslane, Japanese knotweed and the delicate pencilled cranesbill.

Native herbs can also be seen. Wood anemones, wood sorrel, enchanters nightshade, herb bennet and wood sanicle, together with bluebells and primroses. A speciality of the south-west is the three cornered leek, with its garlic-like smell; commonly called a white bluebell it grows alongside roads and lanes. Pennywort grows amongst boulders and on old trees as well as on walls, its clear green particularly noticeable in winter and early spring.

Through the wooded valleys the clear streams flow quickly over gravel stream beds and round large granite blocks. The streams rise in wide marshy areas on the granite uplands, their sources being marked by tussock sedge, purple moor grass and a variety of sedges and rushes.

Moorland

The wildest part of the peninsula must be the upstanding, tor dominated granite hills along the northern coast. Frequently capped by low cloud they brood over the area and send their high rainfall, hurrying down as short streams to the coast. Frost and wind have sculpted and shattered the granite into great angular blocks many of which have accumulated as a scree or 'clitter' around the bedrock granite; while others by various forces have moved down hill and now rest on the lower ground. Many of the boulders are covered with lichen, mosses, ferns and liverworts but soil formation is slow and there is little soil for higher plants.

During the winter months the area is devoid of bird life, but with the warmer weather and the hatching of abundant insects from the boggy areas and temporary pools, some birds do return. Skylarks and meadow pipits share the sky with ravens and magpies, and summer nights on the uplands may be punctuated by the harsh churring of the nightjar which sometimes nests in the granite boulder-strewn uplands. Nightjars, however, are never common birds and only occur as summer visitors.

Unlike other granite uplands in the south-west, no sheep graze this area. The lower slopes are characterised by small, granite hedged fields side by side with derelict fields of bracken and rough grass. On the higher moors the dark peaty soil is sour and hungry, being often highly acidic and poor in plant foods. Natural vegetation cover consists only of woody shrubs such as heather, ling, dwarf gorse and a variety of low growing, acid soil tolerating, perennial plants.

The upland soils are badly drained and wet patches of soil are common. A variety of mosses grow here such as the bog moss sphagnum. This forms the basis for a community of acid water loving plants such as black bog rush, coarse tussocks of purple moor grass and the more delicate bog asphodel and bog pimpernel. Sundew and pale butterwort can also be found here, supplementing the poor nutrient they obtain through their roots, by catching and digesting insects on sticky gland-covered leaves.

Trees are an uncommon sight, particularly on the north coast moorlands, but a few stunted sycamores may struggle to the level of the granite boulders that litter the upper slopes. In slight depressions wind sculpted elder or blackthorn may survive, while lower down the slopes masses of tall European gorse provide nesting sites for wrens, stonechats and yellowhammers.

Imported tree species such as the salt resistant *Pinus radiata*, the Monterey pine, have been planted as shelter belts around some of the isolated high farmhouses bringing a touch of evergreen to an otherwise almost treeless upland.

BADGER leaving the family sett at Treveal.
(J. B. and S. Bottomley)

Visiting and Migrant Birds

Movement of birds takes place during far more of the year than most people realise. The spring migration lasts from March until the end of May, and because those birds which nest above the Arctic Circle only have a short breeding season, the autumn migration begins at the end of July, and continues into the beginning of November. Thus it is that birds are moving for about eight months of the year, and such factors as adverse weather conditions may cause them to move when they would otherwise be resting.

The Land's End peninsula is in an excellent position for anyone wishing to watch for birds on migration. As one of Europe's western extremities, it lies across the migration routes of the Atlantic Coast. Valleys such as Porthgwarra shelter early summer visitors such as chiffchaffs and willow warblers and a wide variety of other warblers and finches on their return from winter quarters in southern Europe and Africa. In the autumn these visitors linger here to take on a final store of food before their long return flight. As the summer visitors leave, birds from the Arctic, northern and eastern Europe are leaving their summer nesting areas to winter in more hospitable temperate climates such as Cornwall's.

There are also many birds which pass through each spring and autumn on their way to or from breeding areas elsewhere in Britain and north-west Europe but which do not actually nest here. Such passage migrants as the nightingale, ring ouzel, skuas, many of the terns, osprey and so on can be seen. These birds are usually found in a similar kind of habitat to that in which they breed, though this is not the rule.

There are often rare and unusual birds here, many are 'overshoot migrants' such as the hoopoe or golden oriole which have travelled too far from their wintering quarters and overshot their breeding grounds in Europe. Others, like the North American long-billed dowitcher or the Asian Pallas' leaf warbler, are real vagrants, having been hurled far from their normal migration routes by adverse weather conditions.

Good places to look for migrant birds are the sheltered valleys which run down to the sea, the edges of muddy ponds and the Drift Reservoir, and from the Island at St. Ives during a north-westerly blow in the autumn, the spectacle of migrating sea birds is superb. Remember though, migrating birds may appear anywhere!

The Check-List

The check-list is arranged by the general habitat in which the various visiting and migrant birds are most likely to be seen, although in such a relatively small area as West Penwith, habitats are bound to overlap.

The time of year at which the birds may be seen is also indicated.

*   Infrequent in West Penwith.
**   Scarce in West Penwith.

SEA CARROT: flowers June-August
(C. Woolf)

Mount's Bay, St. Ives Bay, Drift Reservoir and Freshwater Ponds

The sheltered bays, estuaries and stretches of freshwater provide valuable feeding places for a large number of species.

	Species		Passage Migrant	Winter Visitor	Summer Visitor
	Little grebe	Nov.–Apr.		•	
	Teal	Aug.–Apr.		•	
*	Gadwall	Sept.–May		•	
	Wigeon	Aug.–May		•	
	Shoveler	Aug.–Apr.	•	•	
	Tufted duck	All year	•	•	•
*	Pintail	Oct.–Mar.		•	
**	Scaup	Sept.–Mar.	•	•	
	Pochard	July–May	•	•	
	Goldeneye	Oct.–Apr.	•	•	
*	Long-tailed duck	Nov.–Apr.		•	
**	Velvet scoter	Nov.–Mar.		•	
	Common scoter	Aug.–May	•	•	•
*	Eider	Oct.–May		•	
*	Red-breasted merganser	Nov.–Apr.		•	
*	Goosander	Nov.–Mar.		•	
	Water rail	Aug.–May	•	•	
	Ringed plover	Aug.–Mar.	•	•	
*	Little ringed plover	Apr.–May, Aug.–Sept.	•		
	Grey plover	Sept.–Apr.	•	•	
	Golden plover	Aug.–Apr.	•	•	
	Snipe	Aug.–Apr.	•	•	
	Curlew	July–Apr.	•	•	
	Whimbrel	Apr.–May, Sept.–Oct.	•		
	Bar-tailed godwit	Aug.–June	•	•	
*	Black-tailed godwit	Aug.–June	•	•	
	Green sandpiper	Apr.–May, July–Sept.	•		
	Wood sandpiper	Apr.–May, July–Sept.	•		
	Common sandpiper	Apr.–May, July–Sept.	•		
	Redshank	July–May	•	•	
	Greenshank	Aug.–Mar.	•	•	
	Dunlin	Aug.–May	•	•	
*	Curlew sandpiper	May, Aug.–Oct.	•		
	Knot	Jan.–May, July–Sept.	•		
	Sand martin	Mar.–Oct.	•		
	Reed warbler	Apr.–Oct.	•		•
	Sedge warbler	Apr.–Sept.	•		•
	Kingfisher	July–Mar.		•	

Rocky Shore and Sandy Coves

Including the whole of the coastal margin from St. Ives to Mousehole.

			Passage Migrant	*Winter Visitor*	*Summer Visitor*
	Oystercatcher	All year	●	●	●
	Turnstone	Sept.-Apr.	●	●	●
	Purple sandpiper	Oct.-May	●	●	
	Sanderling	Aug.-May	●	●	
	Common gull	Aug.-Mar.	●	●	
*	Glaucous gull	Nov.-Apr.		●	
**	Iceland gull	Nov.-Apr.		●	
*	Mediterranean gull	Nov.-Apr.		●	
*	Little gull	Sept.-Apr.	●	●	
	Black-headed gull	June-Apr.	●	●	
**	Sabine's gull	Sept.-Nov.	●		
*	Black tern	May, Aug.-Oct.	●		
	Arctic tern	Apr.-May, July-Nov.	●		
**	Roseate tern	May, July-Sept.	●		
*	Little tern	Apr.-May, Aug.-Sept.	●		
*	Sandwich tern	Mar.-May, Aug.-Oct.	●		
	White wagtail	Apr.-May, Sept.	●		

Open Sea

St. Ives Island and Gwennap Head are particularly good vantage points.

	Black-throated diver	Nov.-May	●	●	
	Great northern diver	Oct.-May	●	●	
*	Red-throated diver	Nov.-May	●	●	
*	Great crested grebe	Sept.-Mar.	●	●	
**	Red-necked grebe	Oct.-Mar.		●	
	Slavonian grebe	Oct.-Apr.	●	●	
**	Black-necked grebe	Nov.-Apr.		●	
	Manx shearwater	Mar.-Oct.	●		
**	Great shearwater	July-Oct.	●		
*	Sooty shearwater	July-Oct.	●		
*	Storm petrel	June-Sept.	●		
*	Leach's petrel	Sept.-Nov.	●		
	Gannet	All year		●	●
*	Grey phalarope	Sept.-Nov.	●		
	Great skua	Aug.-Nov.	●		
*	Pomarine skua	Aug.-Nov.	●		
	Arctic skua	Aug.-Nov.	●		
**	Little auk	Nov.-Feb.	●	●	
	Puffin	Apr.-Sept.	●		

Moorland and Clifftop Heathland

			Passage Migrant	Winter Visitor	Summer Visitor
*	Hen harrier	Oct.-May	•	•	
**	Hobby	Apr.-June	•		
*	Peregrine	Oct.-May	•	•	
*	Merlin	Sept.-May	•	•	
**	Dotterel	Aug.-Sept.	•		
*	Short-eared owl	Oct.-Mar.	•	•	
**	Hoopoe	Mar.-May, Aug.-Oct.	•		
	Ring ouzel	Apr.-May, Sept.-Oct.	•		
	Wheatear	Mar.-May, Sept.-Oct.	•		
	Winchat	Apr.-May, Sept.-Oct.	•		
**	Whitethroat	Apr.-Sept.	•		•
**	Richard's pipit	Sept.-Nov.	•		
**	Tawny pipit	Sept.-Oct.	•		
**	Woodchat shrike	May, Aug.-Sept.	•		
**	Ortolan bunting	Sept.-Oct.	•		
**	Lapland bunting	Oct.-Nov.	•		
*	Snow bunting	Oct.-Nov.	•		
	Cuckoo	Apr.-Aug.	•		•
*	Nightjar	Apr.-Sept.	•		•
	Redstart	Apr.-May, Sept.-Oct.	•		
	Black redstart	Mar.-Apr., Oct.-Nov.	•	•	

Valleys and Woodland

In particular the sheltered valleys of Lamorna, St. Loy, Penberth, Porthcurno and Porthgwarra.

			Passage Migrant	Winter Visitor	Summer Visitor
*	Turtle dove	Apr.-June, Sept.-Oct.	•		
**	Wryneck	Sept.-Oct.	•		
**	Melodious warbler	Aug.-Sept.	•		
**	Icterine warbler	Aug.-Sept.	•		
*	Garden warbler	Apr.-May, Oct.	•		•
**	Barred warbler	Aug.-Oct.	•		
	Willow warbler	Mar.-Oct.	•		•
	Chiffchaff	Mar.-Oct.	•		•
	Blackcap	Apr.-Oct.	•		•
	Firecrest	Nov.-Mar.	•	•	
	Spotted flycatcher	May, Aug.-Sept.	•		
*	Pied flycatcher	Apr.-May, Aug.-Oct.	•		
**	Red-breasted flycatcher	Oct.-Nov.	•		
*	Tree pipit	Apr.-May, Aug.-Sept.	•		
*	Yellow wagtail	Apr.-May, Sept.	•		
	Woodcock	Oct.-Mar.	•	•	

Farmland, Hedge and Lane

			Passage Migrant	Winter Visitor	Summer Visitor
	Lapwing	Aug.-Mar.	●	●	
	House martin	Apr.-Oct.	●		●
	Swallow	Apr.-Oct.	●		●
	Fieldfare	Oct.-Mar.	●	●	
	Redwing	Oct.-Mar.	●	●	
**	Nightingale	Apr.-May, Aug.-Sept.	●		
**	Red-backed shrike	May, Aug.-Sept.	●		
'	Brambling	Oct.-Mar.	●	●	
'	Tree sparrow	May, Oct.	●		
	Swift	May-Aug.	●		●

Conservation and the Future

Wildlife needs long periods to adapt to changing conditions and throughout much of Britain changes are taking place that are too rapid for nature to assimilate. In many places plants and animals are threatened by the loss of suitable growing areas, breeding sites and hunting grounds. Against this background, and a growing awareness of the need for conservation, areas such as West Penwith take on a new significance. Despite its rugged appearance, however, the area is vulnerable: changes in farming, the presence of valuable mineral reserves, busy shipping lanes and the growth in tourism all pose a threat.

The traditional pattern of small family farms, predominantly concerned with dairying, has contributed much to the quality and character of the landscape. Farm amalgamation, however, is taking place and means to improve agricultural productivity are constantly being sought. Already some hedgerow removal has occurred; although the protection the traditional hedge gives from the wind and the sheer sturdiness of its construction still outweigh any increased efficiency arising from larger fields.

Perhaps under greater threat are the large areas of uncultivated coastal heathland and high moorland which make up well over a third of the land surface of the peninsula. As we have seen such uncultivated areas are invaluable, both as a support for plantlife and as a source of food and refuge for a vast range of insects, animals and birdlife. The lines of derelict granite hedges criss-crossing these semi-wild areas are, however, evidence of greater farming activity in the past, particularly in the great mining era of the nineteenth century. Now, with rapidly increasing land values and the availability of reclamation grants, the pressure for extending the present margin of farmland into these semi-wild areas is being renewed.

The possibility of a resurgence in mining cannot be discounted, West Penwith is still rich in tin and other non-ferrous ores, the prices of which are rising rapidly on world markets. The old mining industry, which formed the backbone of the local economy for over 2,000 years, left substantial areas covered by derelict buildings and toxic waste, particularly around St. Just and Pendeen. Apart from considerations of amenity, further mining development would require careful control to avoid pollution and disturbance to sensitive areas.

Every year over a million people visit the Land's End itself. Here, in particular, the sheer mass of people has worn away the protective carpet of vegetation and a wide area has been reduced to either bare rock or dusty wilderness. On a smaller scale the cliffs around many of the small coves are also suffering problems of erosion. At Sennen, footpaths in the sand dunes have developed into gaping gashes and, with the undercutting of the exposed sand, the overlying vegetation falls away in great clumps. This leaves an open blowing sand area instead of stable, marram grass-covered, dune.

The clear water and wreck strewn bottom of the shallow coastal waters attract many skin divers each year. Fortunately the British Sub Aqua Club discourage indiscriminate collection of natural history specimens by their members. Other divers, not so responsible, still plunder the now rapidly dwindling stocks of such animals as the large sea urchin. It is, however, from the large commercial collection of specimens for research and teaching purposes that the area could suffer most.

Oil pollution must still be considered the main threat to the area. Since the Torrey Canyon spilled its 14,000 tons of crude oil onto the Cornish beaches and 10,000 sea birds died, great efforts have been made to establish a plan of campaign should the disaster be repeated. We now know that the use of detergent in vast quantities was even more lethal to sea and coastal life than the oil itself. The National Trust policy was always one of caution in the application of detergent and the coastline surrounding their property that was left untreated recovered much more quickly than the dispersant treated areas. The National Trust is responsible for large areas of the cliff and shore and its conservation policies are obviously of vital importance to the future of the magnificent and unique coastline.

The Nature Conservancy Council has in fact stressed that the whole of the Heritage Coast from St. Ives to Mousehole is of special biological, geological and ornithological value— with a major proportion being designated as a 'Site of Special Scientific Interest'. Within this area the Council works closely with landowners and local authorities to maintain scientific values.

The Cornwall Naturalists' Trust Limited maintains a nature reserve at Drift Reservoir. It leases shooting rights from the Water Authority and conserves a woodland area to the north of the reservoir. Members of the Trust also keep a watchful eye on a number of 'Conservation Sites' throughout the peninsula.

Conservation cannot, however, be left to a few organisations. All must be conscious not only of their rights in the free use of West Penwith, but also of their responsibility to ensure that in the future this will remain a magnificent area for both man and wildlife.

LAND'S END. Severe erosion caused by tourist pressure.